A TRUE BOOK™

Dr. Mae Jemison and 100 Year Starship™

Discovering New Planets

T0006884

DR. MAE JEMISON
AND DANA MEACHEN RAU

Children's Press®
An Imprint of Scholastic Inc.
New York   Toronto   London   Auckland   Sydney
Mexico City   New Delhi   Hong Kong
Danbury, Connecticut

Library of Congress Cataloging-in-Publication Data

Jemison, Mae, 1956–
  Discovering new planets/by Mae Jemison and Dana Meachen Rau.
      p. cm.—(A true book)
  Audience: 4–6.
   Includes bibliographical references and index.
  ISBN 978-0-531-25503-2 (library binding) — ISBN 978-0-531-24063-2 (pbk.)
  1. Extrasolar planets—Detection—Juvenile literature. 2. Planets—Juvenile literature. I.
Rau, Dana Meachen, 1971– II. Title.
III. Series: True book.
  QB820.J46 2013
  523.2'4—dc23   2012035762

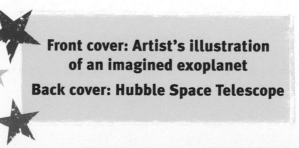

**Front cover: Artist's illustration
of an imagined exoplanet
Back cover: Hubble Space Telescope**

Find the Truth!

Everything you are about to read is true *except* for one of the sentences on this page.

Which one is **TRUE**?

T or F   Our sun is the only star that scientists know for certain has planets.

T or F   It is possible to take photographs of planets located outside of our solar system.

Find the answers in this book.

Contents

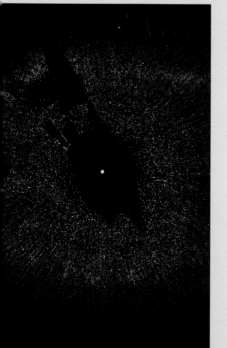

THE **BIG** TRUTH!

Hubble's Planet Picture

How did the Hubble Space Telescope take the first photograph of an exoplanet? **28**

The Hubble Space Telescope orbits Earth.

4 A Closer Look

5 Planets Like Earth

Scientists have found more than 700 exoplanets.

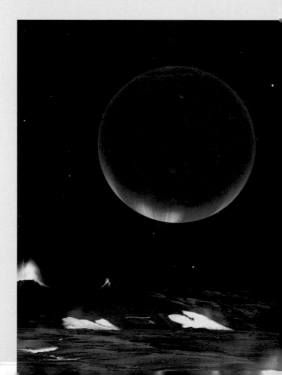

CHAPTER 1

Balls of Rock and Gas

The universe includes everything we can see in the night sky. It includes the space between objects and even objects that are too far away to see. There are huge groups of stars called galaxies. Our universe has billions of these galaxies. Each galaxy contains billions of stars. Our sun is a single star in one galaxy. We call the sun, together with the planets and other objects orbiting it, our solar system.

 Without a telescope, galaxies look like stars when viewed from Earth.

Different Kinds of Planets

The eight planets in our solar system are Mercury, Venus, Earth, Mars, Jupiter, Saturn, Uranus, and Neptune. The planets that orbit closest to the sun are small and rocky. The outer planets are much larger and made of gas. How did such different types of planets form around one central star?

Our solar system contains the eight planets, the dwarf planets, the asteroids, and the comets that orbit the sun.

Mercury Venus Earth Mars Jupiter Saturn Uranus Nept

After the Big Bang, the universe developed to include nebulae, galaxies, stars, planets, and other objects.

Birth of the Universe

Scientists believe that all of the matter and energy in the universe was once packed into an extremely small and hot **particle**. More than 13 billion years ago, the particle started to expand quickly. It pushed its energy and matter out to become the universe. This event is sometimes called the Big Bang. As the very hot matter cooled, it gathered into huge clouds of gases. These clouds are called **nebulae**. Stars were created in the nebulae.

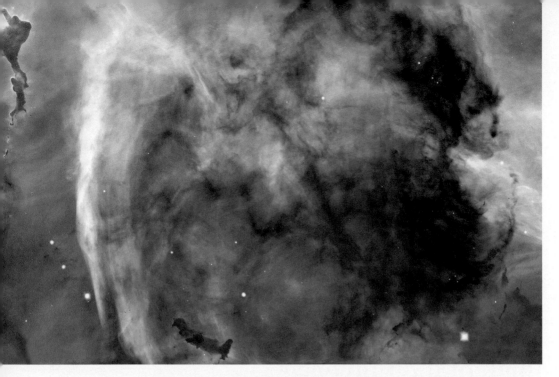

New stars continue to be born in nebulae throughout the universe.

Creating the Solar System

Clouds of dust and gas came together within a nebula. **Gravity** pulled more matter to the center of the cloud. The cloud spun. The center grew hot and started to use the gases as fuel. Scientists think this is how stars form, including our sun. Stars across the universe were created, and are still being created, this way.

Extra matter spinning around the cloud formed into a flat disk shape. Some of the matter in the spinning disk clumped together. And some of these clumps joined together, too. These larger clumps of matter are called planetesimals. Planetesimals are the early forms of the planets.

Planets and other objects developed from the extra matter left orbiting a new star.

Our solar system formed about 4.6 billion years ago.

Forming the Planets

The sun sucked in most of the gases near the center of the disk. As a result, the planets that formed closest to the sun are mostly made of rock and not as much gas. The planets that formed farther from the sun are made of the gas that was still in the disk. As the planets spun around the sun, some crashed into each other. They picked up more matter. The leftover material became moons, asteroids, and comets.

Naming the Planets

Ancient cultures all had different names for the planets. For example, Mars was called Heru-deshet in Egyptian, Mangala in Sanskrit, and Huŏxïng in Chinese. The names we use in the English language today are names of gods in Greek and Roman mythology.

Mercury	Roman god of travel
Venus	Roman goddess of love and beauty
Mars	Roman god of war
Jupiter	Highest of the Roman gods
Saturn	Roman god of farming
Uranus	Greek god of the sky
Neptune	Roman god of the sea

Earth was not named for a god. Earth means "land" or "ground."

Some planets, such as Venus (upper, brighter) and Jupiter (lower), can be easily seen without a telescope.

CHAPTER 2

Searching for Planets

The word *planet* means "to wander" in ancient Greek. Ancient astronomers noticed that some stars in the night sky seemed to wander among the other stars. The planets we call Mercury, Venus, Mars, Jupiter, and Saturn were known by ancient astronomers around the world. Jupiter and Saturn are very far away. Because they are so large, however, they can still be seen without a telescope.

Venus is called the "evening star," appearing as the sun sets and shining the brightest in the sky.

Uranus and Neptune

In the early 1600s, astronomers started using telescopes. They learned even more about the known planets. Uranus could be seen without a telescope, but scientists didn't realize it was a planet at first. In 1781, William Herschel saw it through his telescope. At first, he thought it was a comet. But because it was moving slowly, he realized it was a planet.

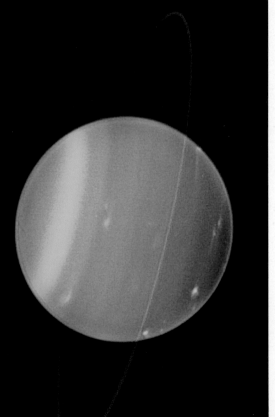

Uranus's rings were not discovered until 1977.

Johann Gottfried Galle used a telescope at the Berlin Observatory to find Neptune.

Scientists found Neptune while studying Uranus. Uranus's orbit was unusual. Scientists noticed that the gravity of another object seemed to be pulling on the orbit. Many scientists tried to pinpoint the orbit of this unknown object. From their data, Johann Gottfried Galle was able to spot Neptune from his observatory in Germany in 1846.

Clyde Tombaugh built many telescop during his lifetime, starting when he was 19 years old.

Clyde Tombaugh was just starting his career at the Lowell Observatory when he discovered Pluto.

Pluto

Pluto was not discovered until 1930. Clyde W. Tombaugh at the Lowell Observatory in Arizona spotted it that year. Scientists were studying the orbits of Uranus and Neptune. Both planets' orbits seemed to be affected by another object. The scientists realized that there must be another planet beyond Uranus and Neptune. That planet, now called a dwarf planet, was Pluto.

Space Probes

Since these discoveries, we have studied our own planets from powerful Earth-based telescopes. The National Aeronautics and Space Administration (NASA) has sent telescopes into space. They have also launched space **probes**. Some probes fly by planets and their moons to take pictures and collect data. Others orbit a planet to study it over a longer period. Some probes land on the planet to study the **atmosphere** and surface.

The New Horizons telescope is scheduled to pass by Pluto in the year 2015.

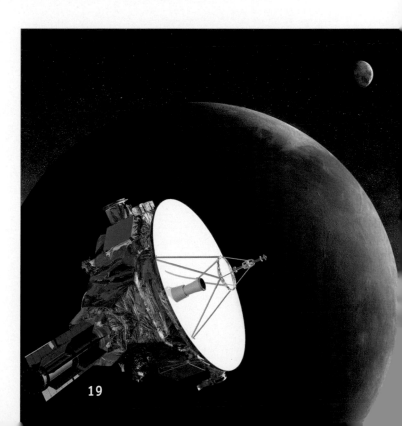

Scientists discover more
exoplanets every year.

CHAPTER 3

Planets Outside Our Solar System

We know a lot about our solar system. But our sun is just one star. There are billions of stars in our Milky Way galaxy. Scientists think it is likely that many of these stars have their own planets. These planets are called exoplanets. It's not easy to find exoplanets. They do not give off light like stars do. They are also too far away for us to see well, even with large telescopes.

There are billions of stars in a galaxy and billions of galaxies in the universe.

Finding Exoplanets

Think of a breeze. You can't actually see it. But you can see a kite using the breeze to fly. You observe the breeze **indirectly**. Just like the discovery of Neptune and Pluto, scientists discover exoplanets indirectly. They observe the behavior of stars that they think may have planets. From a star's behavior, scientists can figure out whether or not it has a planet orbiting around it. They do this using several methods.

A person can observe wind indirectly by seeing how it affects a kite.

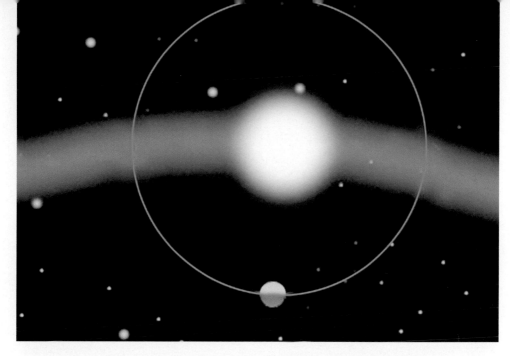

An orbiting planet will make a star appear to wobble because of the planet's and star's gravitational pull on each other.

Radial Velocity

Radial velocity is one method scientists use to study exoplanets. They look for stars that seem to "wobble." This tells scientists that the star might have a planet orbiting it. A star's gravity pulls on the planet orbiting it. As very large planets orbit a star, the planet's gravity actually causes the star to follow a small orbit, too.

Light from stars moving away from Earth shifts toward red. Light from stars approaching Earth shifts closer to blue.

Scientists study systems like this by looking at the star's light. The light appears to be white, but it actually is made up of all the colors of the rainbow. As the star wobbles, it moves farther from and closer to an observer. Its light changes. The star gives off more blue light when it is moving closer and more red light when it is moving away. The larger the planet, the more its gravity makes the star wobble.

Astrometry

Scientists also use astrometry to find exoplanets. They look for a wobbling star. Then they measure the star's position against the **fixed** stars around it. By mapping the star's position over time, scientists can see how much the star has moved. This tells them if it is likely that the star has a planet orbiting it.

Scientists need very accurate measurements from telescopes on Earth and in space to use astrometry.

Transit Method

Scientists can study a planet as it **transits** across a star. This happens when an orbiting planet passes between the star and Earth. Scientists measure how much light the star gives off. When the planet passes across it, the planet blocks some of the light. The star becomes dimmer. The bigger the planet, the more light it will block.

As a planet passes in front of its star, it blocks some of the light from the star.

Scientists blocked part of the sun's light to better see the comets shown at the lower right corner of this image.

Direct Images

Scientists are working on ways to look at exoplanets directly. But it is hard to take pictures of exoplanets. The stars are too bright, and the planets don't give off light of their own. Scientists have developed methods to block a star's light, like a giant shade. They have also developed special telescopes that can work together to reduce the light. Scientists can look at other types of light that planets give off, too, such as **infrared** light.

Hubble's Planet Picture

Scientists find most planets by studying them indirectly. But the Hubble Space Telescope (HST) was the first telescope to photograph an exoplanet in visible light. Astronomers suspected that the star Fomalhaut might have had a planet orbiting it. A ring of gas and dust surrounded it.

Fomalhaut

Astronomers pointed HST to look into this ring. Between 2004 and 2006, the scientists studying images from HST noticed a spot in the ring (small box below).

The spot moved in a path that looked like an orbit. The movement of this spot is shown in the large inset below. Hubble had taken the first photographs of an exoplanet orbiting a star outside our solar system.

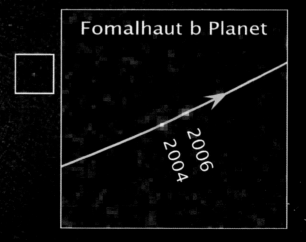

Fomalhaut b Planet

2006
2004

The Canada-France-Hawaii Telescope
(CFHT) was built high on the
mountain Mauna Kea in Hawaii.

CHAPTER 4

A Closer Look

Earth-based telescopes gather data to help scientists find exoplanets. But Earth's atmosphere **distorts** the view. Space-based telescopes orbit above Earth's atmosphere. These telescopes can capture clearer data and images. But stars are very far away. Any changes in their movement or light are very small when observed with telescopes on Earth or in orbit. The equipment used to find exoplanets must have very **precise** measurements.

 Measurements from telescopes may be less than one-thousandth of an inch or centimeter.

Hubble Space Telescope

In 1990, NASA launched the Hubble Space Telescope. HST has taken some amazing photographs of space. It has taught us about galaxies, the life cycle of stars, and the history of our universe. In the search for exoplanets, it has closely studied the gas and dust disks around stars. In 1992, HST found the first exoplanets orbiting a **pulsar**. Since then, many more exoplanets have been found.

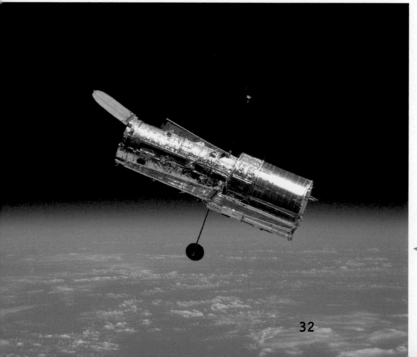

Hubble has found some of the most distant exoplanets ever discovered.

Spitzer regularly sends images and other data back to Earth, then receives new instructions on what data to collect next.

Spitzer Space Telescope

The Spitzer Space Telescope, launched in 2003, measures infrared light. In July 2012, Spitzer recorded a change in the infrared light coming from a star. Scientists believe Spitzer may have found a planet smaller than Earth. Called UCF-1.01, it is a rocky planet that orbits very close to its star. Scientists think its surface temperature could be more than 1,000 degrees Fahrenheit (538 degrees Celsius). That is hotter than Mercury, the closest planet to our sun.

Kepler's mission was planned to last three and a half years, but may last much longer.

Kepler Space Telescope

In 2009, the Kepler Space Telescope was launched into Earth's orbit. NASA uses Kepler to look for Earth-size planets. These planets might be as small as half the size of Earth or twice as big. Kepler is set up to observe the star-filled region of the sky around the constellations Cygnus and Lyra.

Kepler can look at lots of stars at once. It is currently looking at more than 100,000 stars. The telescope uses the transit method to look for exoplanets. It measures the changes in the brightness of stars. The amount the stars' light dims tells scientists the size of the planet and its orbit.

Kepler focused on the same stars, shown in this photograph, for several years.

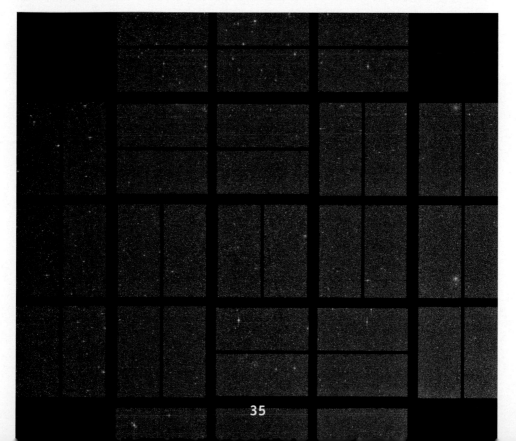

In June 2012, Kepler discovered a star called Kepler-36 with two planets orbiting it. One planet is a rocky planet about 1.5 times the size of Earth. The other planet nearby is almost four times the size of Earth, and is made of gas. This was something scientists didn't expect. How could a solar system form with a rocky planet and a gas planet orbiting so close to each other? Sometimes discoveries bring up even more questions!

The planets orbiting Kepler-36 are so close to each other that one planet can be spotted from the other as easily as the sun or moon is seen from Earth.

Candidate or Confirmed?

Scientists have found thousands of possibilities for exoplanets. Of these, 2,321 are planet candidates. If scientists think that what they're seeing may be a planet, based on data collected by their telescopes, they'll call it a candidate. A planet is confirmed when scientists are able to observe it using two or more different methods. As of 2012, astronomers have confirmed the existence of 729 exoplanets!

Scientists have wondered
for centuries whether
Earth is the only planet
to support life.

CHAPTER 5

Planets Like Earth

People have always wondered about life on other planets. People write science fiction stories, make movies, and play video games about alien worlds beyond our own. Scientists are curious, too. Earth is just the right distance from the sun to support life. The sun's light and heat give us what we need to live. Scientists wonder if similar conditions exist on exoplanets elsewhere in the universe.

Stars seem to twinkle when observed from Earth because our atmosphere distorts their light.

Looking for Life

Most methods that scientists use to find exoplanets are good at finding large, Jupiter-size gas giant planets. But these are unlikely to support life. So scientists are focused on finding more Earth-size planets that may be more like our home. Barnard's star was discovered back in 1916. In January 2012, using data from a space telescope, scientists made an exciting discovery. They found three planets around Barnard's star even smaller than Earth.

Exoplanet Timeline

1584
Giordano Bruno, a Catholic monk, is punished for suggesting other solar systems were likely to exist.

1698
Astronomer Christiaan Huygens writes a book about what life would be like on other planets.

Scientists try to learn if an exoplanet has the right materials for life to exist. The planet would need certain chemicals, such as water, carbon, and oxygen. All life on Earth needs liquid water. So the planet would also need to be the right distance from its star in an area called the **habitable** zone. If it were too close to the star, the water would turn to gas. If the planet were too far away, the water would freeze.

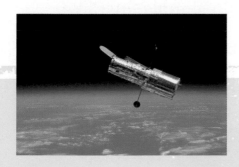

1990
The Hubble Space Telescope is launched from a space shuttle.

1992
Two rocky planets are found orbiting a pulsar.

2009
The Kepler Space Telescope is launched.

A habitable planet needs an atmosphere. An atmosphere keeps water from **evaporating** into space. It also protects the planet from the star's harmful rays. The atmosphere provides living things with necessary gases, such as oxygen for animals and carbon dioxide for plants.

The Search for Extraterrestrial Intelligence (SETI) Institute researchers believe that as beings on other planets advance, they develop radio signals, just like humans did. These signals don't just travel to your home. They go everywhere, including into space.

The sun's light is scattered as it passes through Earth's atmosphere, making the sky appear blue on a clear day.

The Very Large Array is a radio observatory with several radio antennas built in San Augustin, New Mexico.

Scientists at SETI listen to the skies with large radio telescopes. They believe intelligent beings might use radio signals to communicate with us. SETI scientists also study life on Earth. They study extreme areas, such as places with very hot temperatures or without water, to see how living things might survive in different conditions.

Scientists know there are other solar systems besides our own. They learn more every day about these faraway stars and planets. ★

True Statistics

Age of our solar system: 4.6 billion years

Planets known by ancient cultures: Mercury, Venus, Mars, Jupiter, Saturn

Methods to study exoplanets: Radial velocity, astrometry, transit method, direct images

Space telescopes observing exoplanets: Hubble, Spitzer, Kepler

Number of stars Kepler is observing as of 2012: More than 100,000

Number of exoplanet candidates: 2,321

Number of confirmed exoplanets: 729

Did you find the truth?

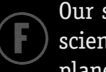

F Our sun is the only star that scientists know for certain has planets.

T It is possible to take photographs of planets located outside of our solar system.

Resources

Books

Halls, Kelly Milner. *Alien Investigation*. Minneapolis: Millbrook Press, 2012.

Kops, Deborah. *Exploring Exoplanets*. Minneapolis: Lerner Publications, 2012.

Miller, Ron. *Seven Wonders Beyond the Solar System*. Minneapolis: Twenty-First Century Books, 2011.

Rau, Dana Meachen. *Aliens*. New York: Marshall Cavendish Benchmark, 2011.

Sparrow, Giles. *Night Sky*. New York: Scholastic, 2012.

Visit the 100 Year Starship Web site at *100YSS.org* for more information on the challenges of travel to another star and ideas on how to solve them. You can also learn about the people who are trying to make the dream a reality!

Visit this Scholastic Web site for more information on discovering new planets:
★ www.factsfornow.scholastic.com
Enter the keywords **Discovering New Planets**

Important Words

atmosphere (AT-muhs-feer) — the mixture of gases that surrounds a planet

distorts (di-STORTS) — twists out of the normal shape

evaporating (i-VAP-uh-ray-ting) — changing into a vapor or gas

fixed (FIKST) — placed or fastened firmly, unmoving

gravity (GRAV-i-tee) — the force that pulls things toward the center of the earth or other object

habitable (HAB-i-tuh-buhl) — safe for organisms to live on

indirectly (in-duh-REKT-lee) — implied or assumed due to its effect, not directly

infrared (IN-fruh-red) — energy whose wavelengths are too low to be seen

nebulae (NEB-yuh-lee) — bright areas made of stars or gas and dust

particle (PAR-ti-kuhl) — an extremely small piece or amount of something

precise (pri-SISE) — very accurate or exact

probes (PROHBZ) — devices used to explore space

pulsar (PUL-sar) — a rapidly rotating star that sends out pulses of energy

transits (TRAN-zits) — moves from one place to another

Index

Page numbers in **bold** indicate illustrations

About the Authors

Dr. Mae Jemison is leading 100 Year Starship (100YSS). This is a new initiative to make human space travel to another star possible within the next 100 years. Dr. J is a medical doctor, engineer, and entrepreneur, or businessperson. She was a NASA astronaut and flew aboard the space shuttle *Endeavour* in 1992. She was the world's first woman of color in space. Dr. J was a college professor, author, and started several businesses. She also works to get more students involved in science. She started an international science camp for students called The Earth We Share. Dr. J enjoys dancing, gardening, and art. She lives in Houston and loves cats!

Dana Meachen Rau is the author of more than 300 books for children. A graduate of Trinity College in Hartford, Connecticut, she has written fiction and nonfiction titles, including early readers and books on science, history, cooking, and many other topics that interest her. Dana lives with her family in Burlington, Connecticut.

PHOTOGRAPHS © 2013: Alamy Images: 18 (Everett Collection Inc.), 40 left (Fabrizio Troiani), 22 (Greg Vaughn), 43 (John W. Warden/Stock Connection Blue), 30 (Masa Ushioda), 14 (Rene Fluger/CTK); Getty Images/Victor Habbick Visions: cover; NASA: 34 (Ames Image Gallery), 35 (Ames/JPL-Caltech), 25 (Caltech/Palomar Observatory), 38 (Earth Day Image Gallery), 4, 28, 29 (ESA, P. Kalas, J. Graham, E. Chiang, E. Kite (University of California, Berkeley), M. Clampin (NASA Goddard Space Flight Center), M. Fitzgerald (Lawrence Livermore National Laboratory), and K. Stapelfeldt and J. Krist (NASA Jet Propulsion Laboratory)), 6 (ESA/A. Zezas (Harvard-Smithsonian Center for Astrophysics)), 5 bottom, 36 (Harvard-Smithsonian Center for Astrophysics/David Aguilar), back cover, 5 top, 32, 41 left (HubbleSite), 3, 8 (Jet Propulsion Laboratory), 19 (Johns Hopkins University Applied Physics Laboratory/ Southwest Research Institute), 33 (JPL-Caltech), 11 (JPL-Caltech/R. Hurt (SSC)), 12 (JPL-Caltech/T. Pyle (SSC)), 16 (Lawrence Sromovsky, University of Wisconsin-Madison/W. M. Keck Observatory), 42 (Marshall Space Flight Center Collection), 20, 44 (MicroFUN Collaboration/CfA/NSF), 41 right (Sandra Joseph/Kevin O'Connell), 27 (SOHO), 10 (The Hubble Heritage Team (AURA/STScI)), 37 (Tim Pyle); Photo Researchers: 24 (David A. Hardy), 23, 26 (Jon Lomberg), 17 (Julian Baum), 9 (Mehau Kulyk), 40 right (Science Source); Shutterstock, Inc./alin b.: 13.